The Victorian Theatre
A Pictorial Survey

This early-Victorian model stage is unusually interesting in showing the backscene divided down the centre so that the two halves could be moved sideways to effect a scene change; this was the regular system in the real theatre where, in Victorian times, the scenes changed without the curtain being dropped. This handpainted backscene is for *Ali-Baba*; the two figures are cut out from one of West's published sheets of characters. (*Model once in the possession of Mrs C. C. Guinness, now in Guildford Museum*)

The Victorian Theatre
A Pictorial Survey

〰〰〰〰〰〰〰

Richard Southern

〰〰〰〰〰〰〰

David & Charles : Newton Abbot

ISBN 0 7153 4968 6

Set in ten on twelve point Pilgrim
and printed in Great Britain
by W. J. Holman Limited Dawlish
for David & Charles (Publishers) Limited
South Devon House Newton Abbot Devon

Contents

Introduction

Queen Victoria's reign lasted from 1837 to 1901. By the twenties and thirties of the present century the words 'Victorian Theatre' had come to mean, for many people, something ponderous and frowsty. When one of the older generation put up such a claim as 'You haven't any actors now like we had in the old days', he would probably have been put down as knowing nothing of the current world of the stage and, worse still, as making sentimental claims for an age that must have been dull because it was, in fact, Victorian!

Today our view has changed. Though we still, quite legitimately, respect the theatre of the first half of our century with all its innovations, we are beginning to discover something of what older men had meant about the Victorian theatre. And that is, that it had some of the most ambitious producers, the most ingenious carpenters, the deepest and most glamorous audience-appeal, the most prolific school of theatre architects, the most outstanding and accomplished scene-painters, some of the greatest tragic actors, some of the most versatile comedians, and—perhaps surprisingly—some of the most widely admired and dazzlingly skilful trick-acrobat-players, that any country has produced in any period.

Comparisons are proverbially odious. This book sets out to describe in quite simple terms what were some of the highest achievements of the Victorian theatre, leaving the reader to study and enjoy them without bothering to compare one age with another. We can, however, make one claim—that any theatre-goer today who went back to the Victorian playhouse could find something somewhere in that vast, glittering picture to catch and hold his attention whatever his taste.

The present opening section is meant to run very quickly over the outstanding points which especially marked the Victorian theatre as different from our own. Such a point, for instance, as its managing all its scene-changes without dropping the curtain. In the sections that follow, a number of facets of the wide subject are taken separately and in somewhat more detail.

The opening illustration on the next page has a double introductory purpose. Firstly, it is almost as fine a portrait of a Victorian auditorium, with all its bad points and all its good points, as it is possible to find in the annals of photography. It was taken by Bedford Lemere, one of the most distinguished architectural photographers of his time. But secondly, it affords a moment's opportunity to make a slight acknowledgement to a branch of the Victorian theatre which the limits of the present book will force us to treat too briefly—namely, that great wellspring of theatrical vitality, the Victorian music-hall.

This picture shows the old Empire Music Hall, Newcastle, as it was in 1891, and more or less as it had stood for over half a century before, from its early days in 1837 at the very beginning of our period. Here are the gold and glitter, the flock wallpaper, the ornament, the benches in the greater part of the house and the 'modern' stall seats in front, the orchestra with its cane chairs, the gracious curves of the circle, and the intrusive but (at that time) indispensable column supports. But above all, the fantastic scenery that belongs to a world of make-believe and waits here ready to be lit up to magic

as soon as the lights go on; the scenery which was regularly changed under the eyes of the audience. All these things introduce us to the Victorian theatre, by way of the provinces before we touch London.

Upon these boards the great figures of Victorian vaudeville poured out their zest and learned their lesson of handling that capricious and incalculable crowd, so simply pleased yet so quickly critical —the Victorian audience.

A particularly striking difference from the theatres of the first half of the present century was that the Victorian fore-stage customarily projected well out into the auditorium, between the side boxes. On the opposite page is a newspaper wood-engraving of the Princess's Theatre off Oxford Street, London, early in our period, specifically in 1843, a few years before Charles Kean was to make this particular house famous throughout the Victorian world for his Shakespearean revivals there (see pages 40-51). The performance here illustrated is of what the newspaper called 'Balfe's new opera of "Geraldine".'

Above on this page is a still more striking example of the Victorian fore-stage and of its power to bring actors and audience into close contact—perhaps surprisingly close. Notice should be given to the actors standing and watching from behind 'in the wings'; to the wing-lights, which lit the side scenery, visible just above the actress's head; and, in front, to the row of shielded footlights so typical of the period (also conspicuous in the picture opposite).

In the Victorian theatre the scenery changed and acted as part of the show. Above is a drawing by William Telbin junior (like his father a master scene-painter), revealing some of the mysteries of the scenes which will be explained in more detail later, on pages 24-35 and 92-7. Particularly to be noticed is the carpenter in the centre helping to pull together the two halves of a 'pair of flats' to effect the scene change, with a fairy at his shoulder standing back from the scene that has just finished, while another fairy rises with her wand through a trap in front to begin the next scene. On the page opposite is a typical example of trick scenery in which part of the scene changed by means of falling flaps. It comes from a set of juvenile theatre prints which faithfully echoed the technicalities of the contemporary stage. In the upper picture a pantomime angler is about to steal a fish from a fish shop. In the lower picture Harlequin waves his hand and two flaps on the central shop fall down to reveal a shop front twice the height, and the punning legend appears—'Extensive Case of Shoplifting'.

12

The two illustrations here, showing both the back and front of the same scene, give a good idea of the make-up of the elaborate set scene which was in several planes. On the Victorian stage there were two distinct varieties of scene, the set scene and the flat scene, and they had different purposes and different effects—indeed, one of the criticisms levelled against Victorian scenery towards the end of the period was that the two different types of effect were mixed indiscriminately in the same show. The flat scene was called 'flat' simply because it was all painted on the flat on a canvas stretched on two great frames, which slid together in grooves and joined at the centre; after use, the picture split up the middle and the two halves were pulled to the sides again out of sight. All this was done before the eyes of the audience in the way shown on page 12. But a set scene on the other hand was much more complicated; it was not flat but made up with several separate cut-out pieces (called set pieces) arranged one behind the other in separate planes. It might even have certain of its details built-out in the round; for example, a cottage porch with climbing roses. The contemporary objection was against having some scenes painted on the flat and some built out in three dimensions in the same show. Every set scene had moreover, in general, to be preceded by a flat scene so that the pieces could be set in place under cover, and then followed by another flat scene so that the pieces could be taken away again. But one could have any number of flat scenes in succession simply by opening or closing the flats. This condition put a great limitation on playwrights, for it meant that they had usually to see that no two elaborate set scenes came together and, consequently, to arrange that a flat scene (or 'carpenter's scene', as it came to be called) should be introduced between them by hook or by crook, to allow of their being changed.

The first of these two pictures shows a model of a set scene made up from parts drawn by one of Charles Kean's scenic artists, Frederick Lloyds, and printed in his book on scene-painting. The separate set pieces of trees, temple, foreground and middle distance are clearly seen against the distant back-cloth. In the second picture this model is viewed from behind with the backcloth removed. Lloyd's ingenious design shows how each separate piece of scenery was constructed and which parts were of canvas (c) and which were cut out in what was called 'profile board' (p). The model has been arranged to show how the hinged arms of the upper grooves (designed to hold the tops of flat scenes) could be pulled up out of the way when a set scene was presented, so enabling it to have a greater height, and exploiting the possibilities of cut and arched upper borders.

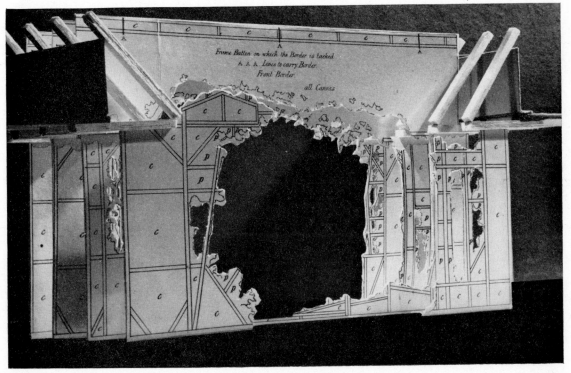

Some Early Victorian Shows

This next section is intended now to give a general view of the range of Victorian shows in the early part of the period. Pantomimes will be glanced at separately on page 36, and the shows of the latter part of the period will be treated on page 82. The range is wide and it is significantly different from the range of early twentieth-century shows. A modern tendency is to say that there was no good Victorian drama. This might be argued. But it seems clear that there were some good Victorian shows. It is an obvious question to ask if any Victorian playwright can be found to compare with Shakespeare. The answer may be 'No', but I think the question itself would be misleading; it ought to be framed: 'Was the presentation of a Victorian play as good from the show point of view as the Victorian presentation of a Shakespeare play?' And the answer here (whatever its limitations) would certainly be 'Yes'. At all events, this section opens with three illustrations from George Scharf's *Recollections of the Scenic Effects of Covent Garden Theatre* (1839). I select first a melodrama (on this page), then one of Shakespeare's late plays and one of his histories (opposite).

The melodrama is Bulwer Lytton's *The Lady of Lyons*. The relevant question is: when, at Covent Garden in 1838, Macready, as the hero Claude Melnotte, exclaimed to Helena Faucit as his wronged wife, Pauline, 'And thou—thou! so wildly worshipped, so guiltily betrayed—all is not yet lost—for thy memory, at least, must be mine till death!' did he move the audience any less than when as Prospero in *The Tempest* (opposite above), he murmured after the masque scene, 'These our actors as

I foretold you are all vanished and are melted into air, into thin air . . .'? Or any less than when, as Henry V before Harfleur, he spoke the famous lines 'Once more unto the breach, dear friends . . .'? (See this page below.) One can obviously do no more than guess the answer; but the old man we imagined on page 7 might well have exclaimed 'He moved them equally whatever he played'.

Turning now to a less controversial subject; there is surely little doubt that, provided one wished to present *Henry V* with full and masterly painting on the scenery, this design (above) by Clarkson Stanfield for the battlefield at Agincourt would submit a claim for very high regard indeed. Stanfield (1793-1867) was one of the first major British scenic artists. He became a Royal Academician, and was noted—even by Ruskin—for his atmospheric effects.

At a completely opposite extreme, the facing page shows something of a particularly characteristic side of Victorian theatre, the staging of celebrated novels. In 1844, five years after Stanfield's *Henry V* drawing, there were four presentations in London of the story which Stanfield's friend, Charles Dickens, had recently finished and which had created almost a new Yuletide custom—*A Christmas Carol*. The reading, and then the theatre-going, public were profoundly moved; and illustrations were given in *The Pictorial Times* of two of these productions, one at the Strand Theatre (above) and one at the Adelphi (below). The moral note in both is strongly emphasised.

A different turn takes us to the five-act costume drama. Here it was not necessary that any particular historic episode should be dramatised; it was simply that a moral melodrama was dressed in period clothes to give it a touch of vicarious authenticity. The illustration opposite is of the play *Honesty* by a 'Mr Spicer'. According to *The Illustrated London News* (4 February 1845), his first piece 'that has been represented at the theatres'. This was at Covent Garden, and George Vandenhoff was in the cast. It undoubtedly offered a moment for broad gesture.

Above is a scene from *The Green Bushes* by J. B. Buckstone who, beside being a versatile player and a manager of the Adelphi and the Haymarket, wrote over seventy plays and burlesques. Incidentally, he also offered a Shakespeare play not in Victorian but 'in Elizabethan fashion'—*The Taming of the Shrew* at the Haymarket in 1844—thus boldly anticipating modern ideas.

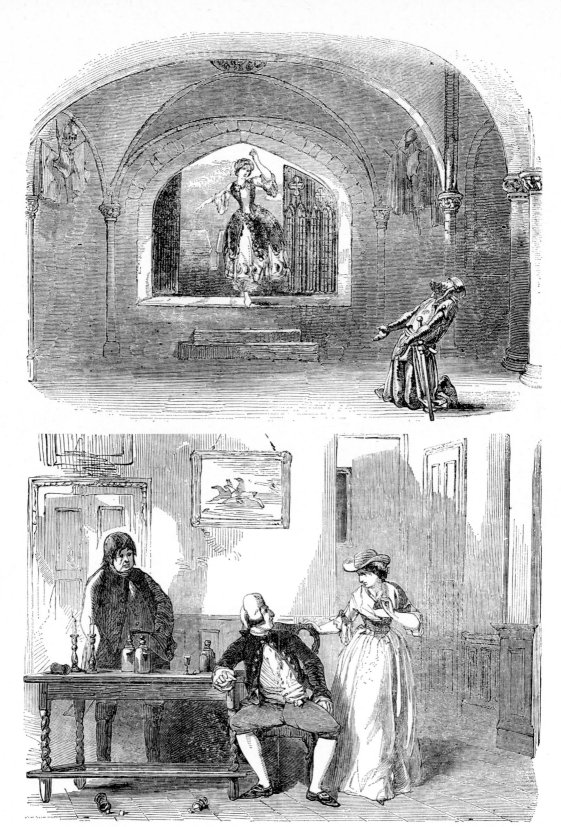

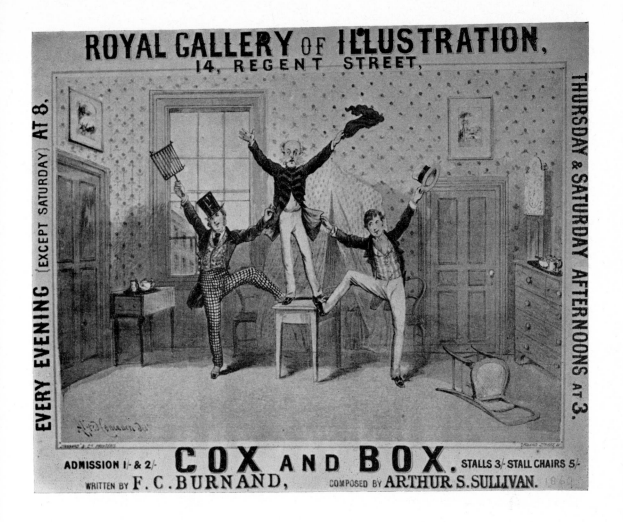

Here are three further varieties of early Victorian show. Opposite above, another historical novel on stage, Sir Walter Scott's *Ivanhoe* at the Haymarket Theatre in 1850; but this time the book is burlesqued. *The Illustrated London News* called it 'the last edition of "Ivanhoe" with all the newest improvements' which 'irresistably excite laughter'. The moment caught in the picture is where the Maid of Judah threatens to throw herself down from the battlements of the Templar's castle. Below: a 'new comic drama' by Mark Lemon, *Mind Your Own Business*, in 1852, also at the Haymarket. The illustration shows Benjamin Webster and Fanny Stirling in a typical scene, where the heroine's sister, Fanny, comes to an inn to rescue the hero (the heroine's rejected lover) from drinking himself to death, upon which he becomes aware that his 'real passion' was for Fanny herself, 'and thus his heart-wounds are at last healed by the discovery of the right object of his love'. (*Illustrated London News* review, 1 May 1852.) Finally, above on this page is something of a curiosity—the advertisement for a musical version in 1867, by F. C. Burnand (later editor of *Punch*) and (Sir) Arthur S. Sullivan, of one of the most famous of all early-Victorian farces—*The Double-Bedded Room* or *Box and Cox*, originally written by J. M. Morton in 1847.

How Victorian Stages Worked

The regular working of a Victorian stage was elaborate enough, as will be seen on page 28, but even in the early days ingenuity elaborated upon this. Some theatres had been built to accommodate horse-racing. Ever since 1770, when Philip Astley had originated his famous 'circus', the English had loved 'equestrian drama'. But horses lose half their appeal if they cannot gallop. At Astley's (and at the early Surrey Theatre) they had galloped round the open 'pit' which, for this reason, contained no spectators and so could not bring in revenue. At the New Standard Theatre in Shoreditch in 1845, however, the horses were kept on the stage, and the pit was filled with audience; but the horses could still gallop. They did so on a moving floor as shown in the picture above, from a newspaper of the time. The proscenium opening here was only thirty feet wide, but the 'equestrian performances' (we read) were 'not given in the area of the auditory, but in the place of the stage; for which purpose the flooring is, by ingenious machinery removed upon a kind of railway . . . and a ring is presented thirty-nine feet

24

in diameter'. Illustrated here is a scene from *The Conquest of Tartary; or, The Eagle Rider of Circassia, and her Monarch Steed of the Desert!* wherein a Mrs R. B. Taylor's performance is very striking...' The 'kind of railway' referred to may have resembled that shown above (though it comes from just after the end of the Victorian period) when, in 1902, *Ben-Hur* was staged at Drury Lane featuring a chariot race with four chariots and sixteen horses. *The Daily Mail* adds that the scenery behind was 'made to travel in the opposite direction at the rate of 1,200 feet a minute'. This was perhaps effective enough, but it is only sprinting a hundred yards in fifteen seconds. The roller-top-desk principle, on which the sections of endless platform where the horses galloped were made, was one very often used in the Victorian theatre—and for an amazing variety of purposes. It consisted essentially of narrow wooden slats glued to a canvas background; it was thus, at once, stiff and yet rollable. It could be used vertically across the stage with a railway train painted on it, to suggest an express rushing by at speed. Or it could be used in a strip, flat on the floor over a 'cut' in the stage, to enable a ghost to rise through a trap and at the same time to drift from stage-left to stage-right as he rose; this was the secret of the 'Corsican' trap (see page 45). The stage name for this flexible surface was 'scruto'.

PLATE I.

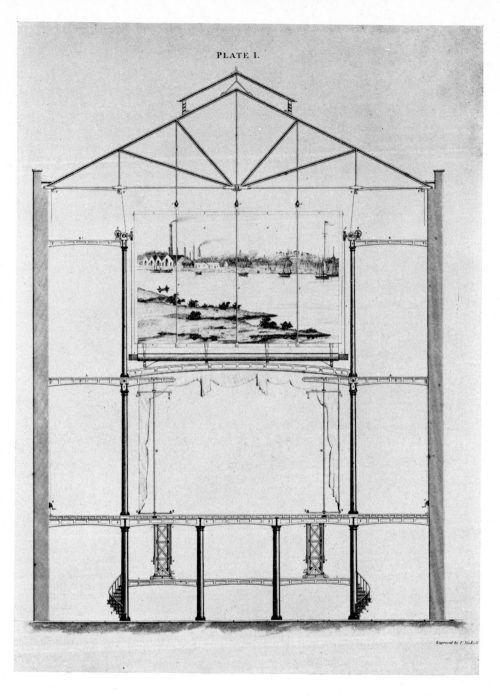

Engraved by F. MacNeill

As a curiosity, typical of Victorian times, may be mentioned another elaboration which sprang, paradoxically, from an attempt to simplify the traditional machinery. An engineer named Stephenson applied, in 1839, for a patent for a scheme of iron machinery designed (as he said in his specification, and his words are worth quoting for the picture they give of the complexities of the Victorian stage) to improve the 'working portion of a large Theatre [which] presents an indistinct chaos of ropes, frames, drums, blocks, windlasses, sheeves, &c. . . . and the number of men requisite for the performance of the varied operations are in proportion, varying from 20 to 50 and upwards, on especial

26

PLATE 2.

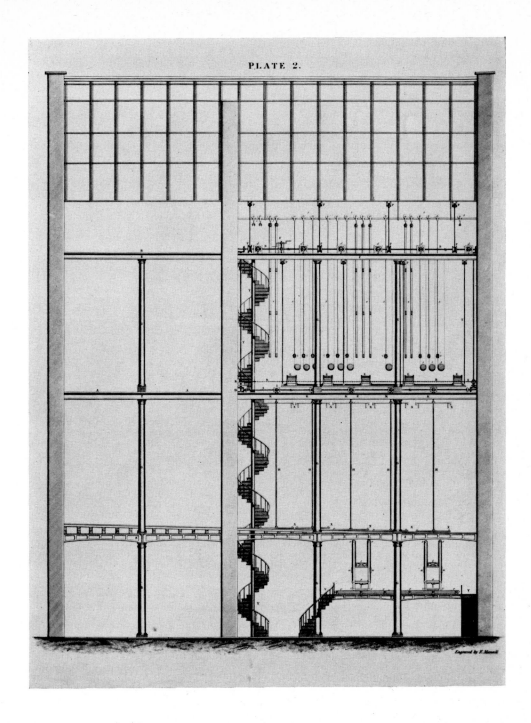

occasions . . . who . . . scarcely ever complete a night's performance without blunders of greater or less extent. . .' His scheme, here illustrated, was put under trial at the Royalty Theatre, Dean Street, for Miss Kelly's production of *Summer and Winter* in March 1840. But, though a horse was called in to help, it proved too heavy to work, and after five nights it had to be totally removed.

Now, after these preliminary curiosities, we may turn to the next page to see what this 'indistinct chaos' of the traditional Victorian stage really was—and for further examples to pages 62 and 63.

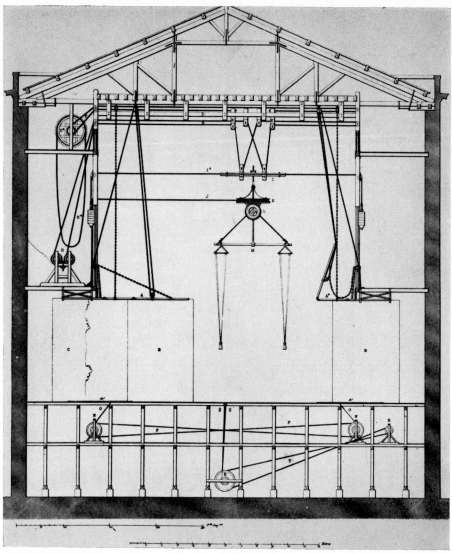

This diagram is from Clément Contant's *Parallèle des Théâtres* published in Paris in 1859, and shows the 'Système anglais'; this is discussed in detail in the present writer's *Changeable Scenery*. (On the continent, however, a quite different system of stage machinery was used.) The special interest of the diagram here is that it shows, nearly half-way up on either side, the sets of projecting grooved arms (A), braced under the fly galleries and supported by chains. It was in these grooves that the tops of the wings (C) and of the separate halves of the flat scenes (B) slid to and fro. When a high set scene was needed the innermost ends of the arms could be raised up on hinges out of the way. (An example of one of these grooves, removed from its working position and put aside, can be seen in the picture on page 62, at the bottom left-hand corner.) Hanging in the centre of the diagram on the present page is a machine for flying effects. The construction of the flats that ran in the grooves is shown opposite; above is a cut flat for a wood scene with, below, a door-and-window flat for an interior scene, both viewed from behind. When the flats joined together they were held in place by two pairs of interlocking wooden cleats, as shown, to keep the pieces flush; but it is only too true that these flats were often badly joined, and the audience has been known to cry 'We don't expect no grammar, but for God's sake join your flats!'

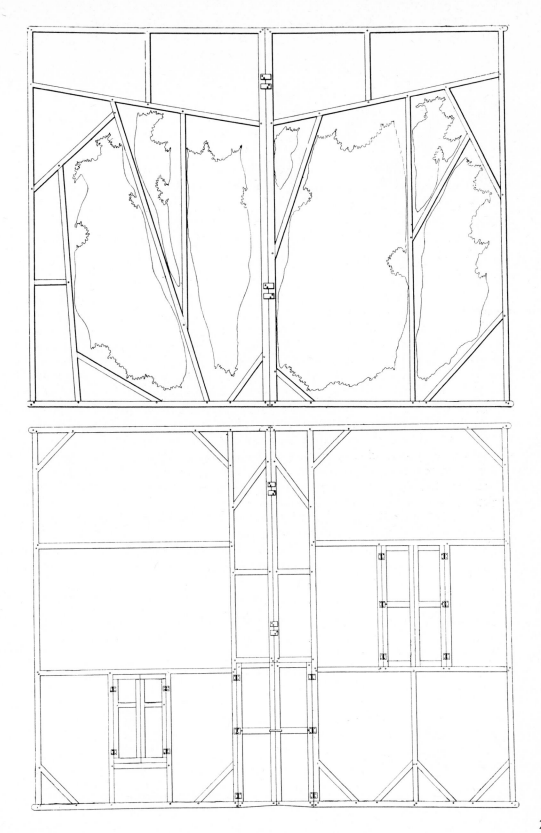

29

Though these pairs of sliding flats were such a regular feature of the Victorian stage, it is curiously difficult to find any picture of them in actual use. Telbin's drawing on page 12 is nearly unique among serious pictorial representations. It would almost seem that some atmosphere of amused toleration, or even of apology, surrounded them in the Victorian mind. They did in fact come in for a good deal of contemporary criticism; the crack down the centre where they joined was repeatedly objected to, especially since it was often begrimed by the dirty fingers of the carpenters who slid them together. Furthermore, the falling into position of the hinged groove-extensions after a set scene, to take the top edges of the closing flats, produced a violent thud, with the clanking of the chains that checked them. And of course a major crisis could come if the flats either jammed in the grooves or fell out of them altogether—which did happen. Or when a flat of one pair was accidentally pushed on opposite a flat of another pair, so that half a wood balanced half a palace ballroom. Thus, one has to dig in obscure corners or turn to comic papers to see them illustrated. For example, the meaning of the cut at the top of this page is likely to be obscure enough to a modern reader. What it in fact represents is two pantomime demons, acting as stage carpenters, and closing-in a pair of scenic flats just as was done in a regular scene-change. The 'scene' they are making is simply a capital letter W at the head of a magazine article. The meaning of the two cuts below might be equally obscure at first sight, but they tell their own story in a Victorian joke that could serve very well as a 'tail' piece to that same article. In the original they bore the simple title 'A Moving Scene'.

On page 31 is a further revealing comment, this time on Victorian amateur dramatics. It comes from *Stage Whispers*, a little book published at the office of the famous comic magazine, *Judy*. The caption

printed beneath runs—'It is rather awkward for the pure Village Maiden while she is saying "I will seek safety in the old cottage", to have to hold it up by the first floor window because someone behind has toppled it over.' But the joke is far from being an impossible absurdity; such accidents happened —even on the professional stage.

The 'pair of flats' was an eminently theatrical convention, which owed its origin to Inigo Jones and the Stuart court masques, but there came a time when the Victorians, advancing towards naturalism, found that it disturbed their atmosphere of 'stage illusion'; and eventually Irving was to do away with them and to replace them finally with the hanging 'cloth' or 'drop scene'.

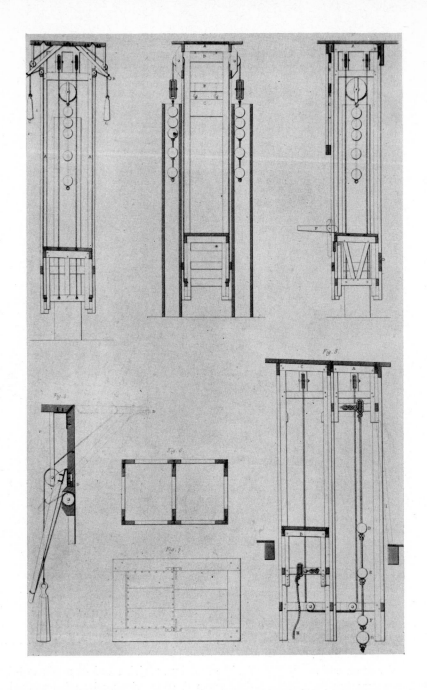

Sinking, rising through the stage, and flying above it were tricks any Victorian master-carpenter might be called upon to arrange for. Traps, as shown on this page from Contant's *Parallèle*, were designed with the greatest ingenuity, and would be differently made for different effects. The three shown at the top of the illustration are for instantaneous appearances through the stage with a high leap (as seen for example on page 108), and the one shown below is for the sudden substitution of one character for another. Aerial effects included grouped flights out over the audience as in the sensational example opposite, showing Kellar's 'Levitation, from stage to dome without mechanical appliances' [*sic*]! This belongs to the latter part of our period when tricks approached the degree of a fine art.

32

Two extremes of skill in tricks are shown here. Above is a capital letter T from *Punch*, about 1852, designed to illustrate the astonishing agility of the acrobatic player in using a 'leap trap', that is, a pair of hinged flaps in the scenery through which the actor disappeared with a single jump. The degree of skill and precision demanded for this sort of work gave rise to something like a hereditary craft confined to certain specialist families. Opposite is a diagram from *The Sphere* of 1901 announcing the installation of 'five new electrically controlled bridges' in the stage of Covent Garden. In the floor of the two bridges nearest the orchestra can be seen traps for the appearance of characters in the traditional way from lower floors specially built below on the same bridges. The theatre shown here is that built by Barry in 1853 (and illustrated below on page 75), as a comparison of the small section of side boxes glimpsed on the left of the present picture will show. The whole of the stage and some parts of the auditorium were reconstructed in 1901 by E. O. Sachs (who wrote *Modern Opera Houses and Theatres*, possibly the largest study ever made), to keep up with the changing times; and what had formerly been a 'fixed' stage was now entirely rebuilt so as to be capable of rising or sinking in sections, to offer mountains or ravines, balconies or cellars, far beyond the resources of such a modest stage as that shown on page 28. The innovations might be of little use in the advancement of dramatic writing but they presented a suitably expensive tool for the re-creation of grand opera.

34

THE OLD STYLE OF SCENE-RAISING
The vanished wooden flies at Covent Garden Theatre on which the old scenery used to be raised

THE NEW STYLE OF SCENE-RAISING
Showing the new mechanism above the "gridiron" for raising and lowering the scenery at Covent Garden

A Glance at Pantomime

So far as elaborate trick entertainment went, the Victorian Christmas pantomime became one of the wonders of its time. Here and on the next two pages are shown eight of the pantomimes presented in London about the mid-century—no less than seven of them being staged in the same year, namely 1851. The first illustration comes from Drury Lane in 1843, when *Harlequin and King Pepin; or, Valentine and Orson* was presented as an afterpiece in the same programme as Weber's *Der Freyschütz*—so contributing to a veritable feast of effects. The scene shown is the discovery by King Pepin of one of the 'babes' in the forest, while his army marches past behind the groundrow in true pantomime fashion. Below on this page follows the first of the 1851 pantomimes, that at Drury Lane, of *Harlequin Hogarth; or, The Two London 'Prentices* with a typical scene in a shop surrounded by an elaborate balcony.

At Sadler's Wells in the same year the management under Greenwood presented *Harlequin and the Yellow Dwarf; or, The Enchanted Orange Tree and the King of the Golden Mine* (above), with scenery by the distinguished resident scenic artist, Frederick Fenton. Note the false heads, and the giants painted on the backcloth. At the City of London Theatre in Norton Folgate, Nelson Lee presented at the same time *Oliver Cromwell; or, Harlequin Charley over the Water and the Maid of Patty's Mill* (below), the reference being to King Charles I, whom the illustration shows hiding in the oak tree.

Many of the pantomimes were highly topical in treatment but that at the Adelphi in the same year was called simply *Little Red Riding-hood* (above), and *The Illustrated London News* almost with a touch of surprise remarked that 'the management here have gone no further than the nursery for a subject'. The pantomime at Astley's, however, naturally made a great feature of its equestrian tradition and included horses, and even ostriches. It was entitled *Mr. and Mrs. Briggs; or, Punch's Festival* (below). It should be noted that horses are even represented in the clouds round the aerial globe.

The Princess's Theatre in the same year turned nautical and presented the pantomime of *Harlequin Billy Taylor; or, The Flying Dutchman and the King of Raritongo* (above). A ship scene was a favourite subject on the Victorian stage, and its typical make-up is described in the details on page 96. This scene from *Harlequin Billy Taylor* was in all probability constructed in just this way. At the Surrey Theatre the pantomime was *The King of the Golden Seas* (below), again featuring the Victorian pantomime convention of artificial 'big-heads'.

A brief word must be given to one especial marvel of the pantomime. Every plot was so devised that at the crucial moment a complete metamorphosis of the whole scene took place visually—by means of transparencies, rising and falling gauzes, opening pieces, 'rise-and-sinks', etc to provide a crowning miracle of effect.

The Great Charles Kean Revivals

The Princess's Theatre (which stood just on the north side of Oxford Street) was the site, from 1851 to 1859, of one of the outstandingly typical masterpieces of the mid-Victorian theatre—the seasons of revivals of Shakespeare plays (and also the production of certain 'gentlemanly melodramas') by Charles Kean and his wife Ellen Tree. These created a fashion in presentation that lasted till the end of the Victorian era.

Spectacular scenic effects marked all Kean's productions. He was willing to incorporate all the newest stage techniques into his Shakespeare. For instance, in *A Midsummer Night's Dream* (1856) he staged the lovers' wandering through the woods with the help of a moving diorama as background; for its design by Thomas Grieve, see above. He also included at the psychological moment a complete ballet of Amazonian soldiers and an avenue of flower-arches held up by fairy dancers, together with flying effects (see opposite). The word 'diorama' seems to have been used to name a panorama in two planes; a panorama was an all-embracing view painted on a very long canvas, unrolled from one vertical end-roller to the other, so presenting a sliding picture. This formed one of the great artistic-cum-educational pastimes of the Victorian era, and might be accompanied by music and a lecture. A diorama (at any rate in the sense in which Fenton used the word at Sadler's Wells) was two of these rolling views, one in front of the other, with intervals in the first cut out to show the other behind—giving an effect much like the 'multiplane' effect of a Disney cartoon.

Another outstanding feature of Kean's presentations was the company of brilliant scene-painters he assembled—F. Lloyds, the Grieves, W. Telbin, W. Gordon and others—using as many as he thought suitable in one show. A great collection of water-colours of the scenes they produced is now preserved in the Theatre Collection of the Victoria and Albert Museum.

41

Above is another of the scenes for *A Midsummer Night's Dream*, designed by Gordon in true romantic-classical tradition. Opposite, above, is a windmill on a stormy hill from the brush of Frederick Lloyds (who wrote a treatise on his art, entitled *Practical Guide to Scene Painting and Painting in Distemper*, about 1875, concluding with a chapter headed 'Method of Painting a large quantity of Flowers in a rapid and effective manner'). The windmill scene was designed for a production of *King John* in 1852, and by any standard is a fine piece of free and vivid technique.

Below, opposite, is an example of the meticulous care in reproducing a perspective-architecture scene. It represents the interior of a palace in *A Winter's Tale*, and was the subject also of a distinguished continental juvenile theatre sheet.

43

The Corsican Brothers (1851) was an example of Kean's 'gentlemanly melodrama'. Like the other shows, it exploited trick effects. Above is the scene of a chateau-interior with a transparency background, where one of a pair of twins telepathically sees his brother in a duel, which duel is actually portrayed as a vision behind the transparency gauze, as shown below.

In the second act the same action is seen again but now from the point of view of the other twin. This upper picture shows the snowbound forest where the duel took place, and the lower shows the vision experienced by the vanquished twin as he lay bleeding in the snow and saw his brother thinking of him at home in the chateau. It was for this play that one of the most famous traps in theatre history was devised—the 'Corsican' trap.

46

A further striking feature of Kean's work was his extensive search for correct topographical detail. His *Merchant of Venice* (1853) contained a view of that city by William Telbin that was both recognisable and brilliant (opposite, above). It was built on the stage with practicable bridges, and boats moving in the canal, and became alive with people in a special carnival scene (opposite, below). On this page is a photograph of Drinkwater Meadows as Old Gobbo in this play. He joined with Kean in the management of the Princess's, but the particular interest of his photograph in the present context is that behind him can be glimpsed what is apparently a part of this actual scene of Telbin's on the stage, which makes the picture very unusual indeed as an early record.

Turning for a moment from the detailed watercolour records which Kean had made of his own shows, the picture above illustrates how the contemporary newspaper saw his productions—specifically the queen's dream-scene in *Henry VIII*. The cutting is from *The Illustrated London News* of 2 June 1855, and shows a transparency gauze in the back wall of Queen Katherine's chamber, by means of which it was possible to show to the audience the actions of her dream in 'reality'.

Beyond all these things, Kean was a great innovator in the teasing study of 'archaeological exactness'. He himself was a Fellow of the Society of Antiquaries, and he employed the most distinguished specialists of his day to guide him in the design of his historical details.

Opposite above, is a scene designed by Lloyds for Kean's *King Lear* (1858). The 'French tent' and its bed are drawn with great care for detail. But this general scheme was not enough; in order to guide the property-maker more exactly a separate study of the bed and tent-hanging was made, as shown below. This is but one example of a care for detail that went so deep that designs were made and coloured for even such simple items as the straight wands carried by court officials in *A Winter's Tale*. (It is interesting to note in passing that in the latter production the part of the child, Mamillius, was played by a little girl whose name was Ellen Terry.)

49

D

Thomas Grieve produced, for this same *King Lear*, a highly imaginative and convincing design for one of the blasted heath scenes (above). And it is perhaps with a little surprise that we turn from this to see (opposite) a photographic portrait of Kean himself in the role of Lear. It is marked by a quality of what we today might call 'theatricality' in a slighting sense. But it does convey something of the effect made by Kean in mixing audience-appeal (that is, appeal to the audience of those days) with his various other qualities mentioned above, so as to provide for the Victorian theatre-goer and his family (for up to that time it had hardly been respectable for a man to take his family to the theatre) a feast of spectacle, sentiment, scholarship, education and some Shakespeare, in a total unity that could hold Queen Victoria spellbound.

But it was only '*some* Shakespeare'—not all; for the elaboration spent on the scenery, and the additional ballets and effects, took up so much of the night's performance that the script had to be extensively cut and rearranged to be included at all.

The Social Life of a Provincial Theatre

Almost by chance, it seems, a piece of unusual good luck helps us to reconstruct what I may call the 'social life' of a provincial Victorian theatre, with a surprising vividness. There survives a set of magic-lantern slides made just before the demolition of the old Theatre Royal, Birmingham, which recapture the atmosphere of the theatre and suggest what it might mean to the people of the time. The theatre in Birmingham

opened in 1774 and finally closed its doors in 1901. Originally it had a sophisticated Georgian-classic facade, as shown in the print from *The European Magazine* at the top of this page. Below is a view of that same facade just before it was pulled down. The changes in the details of the architecture illus-

trate the transition from a fastidious age to an industrial age, whose burden of smoke and fog is already closing down. The picture is taken from Bennett's Hill; if we could now walk into the side street where the old entrance to the gallery was, we should see the view reproduced above. There could scarcely be a better justification for the existence of that quality of Victorian theatre which brought warmth, red plush, gilt, glamour and temporary escape to the factory-worker of Victorian England. The surviving poster advertises *Sweet Nell of Old Drury* beside Bass's Pale Ale, while under the fog, the doors to the 'gods'—the highest and cheapest seats in the theatre—wait as if to open again to a session of the magic of the theatre.

The three views on pages 54 and 55 are well worth preserving for the story they tell of the world in which the Birmingham Theatre Royal worked. The first of them shows the side view of the main facade as seen from New Street, among its surrounding shops, while below, between a grocer's and a tavern, are the double doors of the pit entrance in Lower Temple Street, with the vaulted roof of the great station in the background echoing the industrial feat of the Crystal Palace. On this page is a rare piece of sunlight and shade, illuminating a close-up detail of the same entrance—that leading to the next most expensive part of the house after the 'gods'—namely the pit. Coming before such doors, and from such streets, one could well visualise the thrill of anticipation that a prospective visit to a theatre might arouse in those days. Contrast would be the essence of the experience.

Adjoining is a long view of the bearded and moustached spectators at Bragg's Bar in New Street; below, a glimpse of 'Bragg's Wine Cellar, Theatre Royal'.

As a sort of catalytic agent to the glamour of the Victorian theatre was the gin palace or wine cellar or bar, with the atmosphere recorded opposite. Here was an influence for good or bad, but clearly one whose effect was to add glamour to the gilt-and-plush magic of the performance, and to offer a further inducement to the Victorian male (it should be noticed that no women are to be seen in these pictures) to throw off the concerns of his day's work and the squalor of his streets. Notice the sheaves of play-bills and portraits on the walls of the bar, and the momentary fixedness of the spectators as they themselves become for a flash the actors in a 'living drama' for our entertainment (and instruction).

Above, on this page, is the reverse of the coin. Here is the nearly-ceremonial stairway, in front of the house, to the circle—one of the most coveted viewpoints in the theatre. Here are combined lace curtains, portraits, decorative ironwork, a (very necessary) door mat, drugget to protect the luxurious carpet, flock wallpaper, bright lights, and even an aspidistra. It was in these surroundings that the manager would stand nightly in evening dress and extend a genuine, homely welcome to the patrons of the more expensive seats.

For the players, the atmosphere was different; a little more of the seamy side crept in. But for the favoured ones there was still a touch of special treatment even here as was only right, for the appeal in a 'star' name might fill the theatre. Behind the scenes the surroundings were certainly not glamorous, as this picture of the stairway up to the dressing-rooms shows. The actors picked their way through packs of flats all waiting to be run-on to the stage to take their place in some stock scene.

But once in his dressing room (see opposite above) the 'Star Gent' had some pretensions to respect and comfort. A valance hid the legs of his dressing-table, and though the carpet was worn and the paper dado peeling a little from the walls, his mantlepiece might hold a bottle of gin; and a thoughtful —or prudent—management added a notice above to the effect that the circle bar would be open 'for half an hour after the fall of the curtain for the convenience of THE ARTISTES'.

The 'Star Lady's' room, with a draped cheval mirror in the corner, was even more gracious (see opposite below).

After such preliminaries, the impression of the auditorium (above) seems at first a little bare and humdrum. Despite the attempts at elaborate decoration, the seats are no more than padded benches, and the circles are supported on bare columns which would certainly have impeded the view of several of the spectators. While the audience was assembling, the costumed actor, ready to serve them,

would wait in a 'Green Room' (left) which, despite certain drawbacks, was a superb example of contemporary decoration. Here too, the management hung the notice offering the courtesy of the circle bar to the players.

When at length the curtain rose, however, the old magic of the stage-scene dominated the picture, and theatre glamour held sway before the darkened auditorium. (The custom of dimming the house-lights came in with the installation of gas in theatres about mid-Victorian times.) Notable examples are shown here (see above) of 'profiled tree wings' and of 'cut foliage borders' with a 'forest backcloth' behind. Notice the fashion of a hugely high architectural arch to the proscenium opening, which practical considerations always demanded that the stage carpenter should cut down to about half its height, by means of a great 'pelmet proscenium border'.

Penetrating now into the world of technicalities, we may climb to the upper 'fly floor', whence the ropes that held the hanging scenery were worked. These 'floors' were in fact galleries running above either side of the stage. In the picture above, are seen some of the set of 'drums and shafts' by which 'borders' (or top scenery) were worked. Especially interesting is it to see, in the lower left-hand corner, a rare example of a dismantled scenic 'groove', with its armed extension folded back (compare pages 12 and 28). Above on the opposite page is the lower fly floor, to the rail of which the ends of the working-lines are cleated. Below, is a picture of the 'thunder run', a sloping wooden trough down which iron balls were rolled to simulate a storm. And very effective they were.

We leave the Birmingham theatre with a glance at two specialist departments. Above is shown the domain of the resident scene-painter, his smart suit protected by an apron, his huge palette in front of him, and beyond it, the great rising and falling frame on which the scenes were stretched to be painted (see also pages 90 and 91). A second frame is behind him. The scene-painter in those days was a figure of considerable importance in the theatre, being both designer and executant in one; he was frequently a master of the delicate technique of distemper, or size-bound paint, which he mixed him-self as he went along, and used hot. Furthermore he was sometimes called on to design and paint the decoration of the auditorium (and even has been known to write the script of the Christmas panto-mime). Below is the department of the lighting expert—the 'gas man' in the days before electricity and for some time after, while electricity was being first used in theatres. A complex of gas pipes and control valves is seen at the left, and a demon-mask with electric eyes on the shelf at the back.

E

Victorian Audiences

In this section we turn from the study of a particular theatre to look briefly at the Victorian audience as a whole; and the impression is mixed. The pictures here mostly explain themselves. It was in the 1850s that the chief social development of the Victorian theatre took place. Before then the theatre had had a reputation for rowdiness; no decent lady should be seen in it; its seating and appointments were spartan and subject to much ill-usage. But during the fifties a certain aura of respectability began slowly to creep in, and some degree of comfort and even luxury came with it. The taking of tickets at the box office became dignified (see above) and evening dress became common in the stalls (see left), where we have incidentally a glimpse of a curious entrance to the stalls by way of the back of the pit.

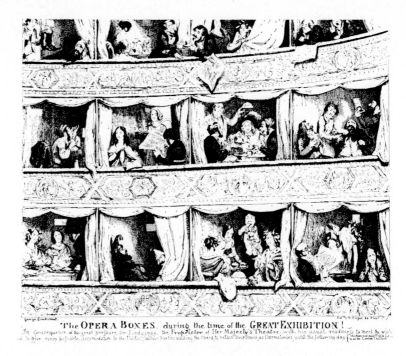

The tiers of side boxes at the opera took on a drawing-room atmosphere; at the time of the Great Exhibition, George Cruikshank even caricatured them as offering to meet the convenience of the great crush of visitors to London by remaining open all night! (See above.) Below, in a more serious mood the same artist records an occasion in 1854 when the audience at Sadler's Wells passed on to the stage, by means of a bridge over the orchestra, to sign the Total Abstainer's pledge.

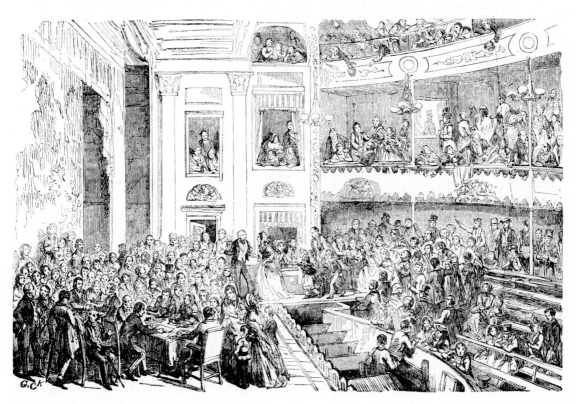

BOXING-NIGHT - A picture in the National Gallery.

But Cruikshank had a different story to tell of the occupants of the typical gallery (the 'gods'), and represented them with all their old rowdiness (above). Fred Barnard, in the sixties, showed that the situation was slow to improve (below).

The Royal Victoria Coffee Palace and Music Hall in the New Cut, near Waterloo Station, later became the famous Old Vic; in the eighties it was already catering for its popular audience in a special way by offering them temperance drinks, coffee and tea, sausages and potatoes, 2d and 3d (above). Not only were women now to be seen partaking, but a father might bring his small children here for refreshment while he sat and read his paper under the tea urns.

A very different atmosphere was created in the great foyer at Covent Garden, where the social amenities were also maintained but at a level approaching the palatial, with great mirrors, rich curtains, and brilliant gas chandeliers (see below).

Something of a similar development took place in the character of theatre architecture, as the following section will show.

Victorian Theatre Architecture

The bareness of the typical small provincial playhouse of the 1830s is very well portrayed in these two pictures of 'Fisher's Theatre' at North Walsham, just north of Norwich (opposite). Hard backless benches (whose covering was traditionally green baize) were in all parts of the house, whether gallery, pit or boxes. The view of the stage illustrates well the two 'doors of entrance' for the actors, which were a legacy from Restoration and Georgian times. The festoon drop-curtain (also of green baize) worked just upstage of these doors, leaving a more or less deep fore-stage for 'front scenes'. Notice the fewness of the 'ornamental' gas brackets round the circle front, which were the sole illumination of the auditorium.

The contrast between such a theatre in the thirties and Drury Lane at the end of the Victorian period is great indeed, as can be seen by the excellent photograph by Bedford Lemere on the following two pages. Drury Lane had its accidents, however, in the intervening decades, as when the cornice of the colonade, where the queues still stand today down the side of the theatre, fell to the ground on 11 July 1875, as shown below. Within the auditorium, the supporting pillars still remained to prop up the galleries (before the application of the cantilever system) and they could be seen as late as the 1920s, to which the photograph on pages 72-3 belongs.

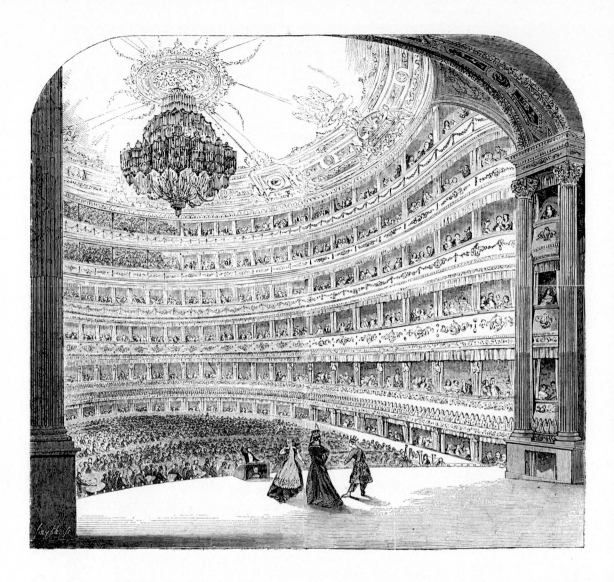

These two pages contain a brief history of Covent Garden during the period. In 1847, great alterations were made to the interior to transform it into the Royal Opera House, by which name we know it today. The illustration above shows the immense new auditorium with its six tiers of boxes.

One interesting feature of Georgian and Victorian theatre architecture was that both large and small theatres were so designed that the pit could be floored over level with the stage—thus affording a large area on occasion, suitable for dances and so forth. In 1856 an occasion of this sort was being celebrated at Covent Garden when fire broke out (see opposite above), and the building was destroyed.

Opposite below, is a newspaper picture of the new Opera House which followed in 1857, designed by the architect, E. M. Barry, and which—with some modifications—remains as the building we know today.

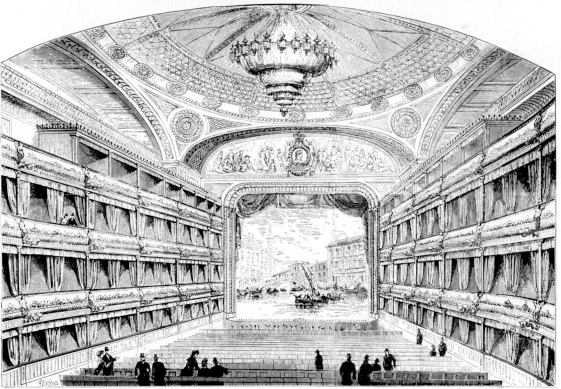

The chief contrast illustrated opposite is between the kind of theatre that was still being built about 1850, as exemplified in F. W. Bushill's design for the Olympic Theatre in Wych Street, in the old tradition (above), and that built by T. H. Wyatt, known as the New Adelphi, in the Strand some eight years later to replace the earlier Adelphi. The contrast is in the matter of physical comfort; the Olympic retained much of the past spartan tradition of wooden benches, while the New Adelphi (below) was among the first London theatres to evoke from the press of the time the epithet of 'luxurious'. A new era was beginning; in most general respects of disposition the two houses are similar, but in the details an entirely new scale of comfort and decoration is offered by the Adelphi. The act-drop seen in the picture was designed by Clarkson Stanfield.

Above on this page may be seen the appearance in the seventies of a theatre whose name today has become synonymous with the most modern experiments of the new dramatists—The Royal Court Theatre, Sloane Square. Originally sited on the south side of the square, it was reconstructed as shown here by the architect, Walter Emden, for Marie Litton in 1871, and later housed the first Pinero farces. In 1887 it was demolished, and the present theatre on the east side of the square opened the following year to replace it.

The elegance of the fashionable west-end theatre of the eighties, and the downrightness of the theatre of the people at the same period are nicely contrasted in the drawings on these two pages.

The picture above shows the Princess's Theatre in 1880, but it is a different building now from that which Charles Kean had made so famous in the 1850s, as a glance back at page 10 will show. Kean may have suffered criticism for his over-decoration of Shakespeare but he brought elegant society into his theatre. The building had to change to suit; its ornateness here is almost royal, the trimmings (and dust-traps) profuse. The fore-stage has shrunk. Formal dress and social manners mark the little character-sketches of spectators to be seen taking their seats in preparation for the rise of the fabulous curtain with its royal coat-of-arms.

The other side of theatre-going, however, is portrayed in the two pictures below of the Royal Victoria Hall in 1881. Pipes are here conspicuous in the pit, and the majority of the men are actually wearing their hats. The decoration of the auditorium has admittedly some pretention to gaiety—but nothing to be compared with the Princess's. A music-hall act is being presented on the stage. It is perhaps not by chance that an earnestness is shown in this audience which has certainly not yet settled down on the spectators in the opposite page. The Victorian 'haut monde' and the Victorian 'London poor' now had their separate theatres.

The Victorian theatre buildings are now almost all swept away or modernised to suit twentieth-century fashions. One very typical example was, however, caught by the camera before it vanished from the public eye, and the photographs offer a fitting conclusion to this section. In 1897-8 the Granville Theatre was built on a corner of The Broadway, Walham Green, in the borough of Fulham. It was designed by one of the most experienced of Victorian theatre architects, Frank Matcham. It was free from the nuisance of supporting columns; the bold, sweeping lines of its galleries are particularly sensational (see above); and the architect introduced an interior finish intended to provide something more hygenic than the dusty draped curtains, fringes and painted plaster modelling of (for instance) the Princess's Theatre (page 78), but something that, at the same time, had to allow of all that elaborate relief work which seemed indispensable to the Victorian idea of an auditorium. He settled on the novel solution of a decorative scheme carried out in 'Eburite faience tiles' (see opposite and above). The result was perhaps reminiscent of an old-fashioned milk-shop interior but the glitter and glamour of the age were still there. All the same, this theatre stood for an age in entertainment that was beginning to fade away. About the late 1950s, after a period of disuse, a move was made to transform it into a television studio, but as a theatre its days were over.

F

Some Late Victorian Shows

Sensationalism as a fine art began to mark the shows of the second half of the nineteenth century. Electricity came slowly into general use in theatres (it was dangerous, and its fire-risk is considerable on the stage even today), and it was not common until the eighties, but already in 1849 Her Majesty's Theatre in the Haymarket staged a 'new ballet' called *Electra; or, The Lost Pleiad*, of which the above picture shows the culminating impressive effect with Carlotta Grisi as the central figure 'darting out

that intense light so long the secret of nature, and which is the one luminous power to eclipse the traditional light of gas'. The waterfall effect of *The Devil's Ring* at Drury Lane in 1850 (below) was however a common thrill, and perhaps in this production it was too commonly treated, for *The Illustrated London News* called it 'particularly deficient' in 'the sense of illusion'. The Victorian papers were exceedingly critical of the shows of their time.

On the other hand, the shipwreck scene (above) from *The Chain of Events* at the Lyceum (1852, with Charles James Mathews, husband of Madame Vestris) evoked high praise for its staging—when the ship sank 'it was terrible. The shriek of the audience almost substituted that of the crew!' But the critic was most lukewarm about the plot. In *The Courier of Lyons* or *The Lyons Mail*, at Kean's Princess's Theatre in 1854 (below), by Charles Reade, the audience could see the outside as well as the inside of the inn and 'thus a double action' could be presented (the window to the right was a transparency). *The Illustrated London News* commented dryly, 'In the higher drama, this would suggest a want of art . . . with melodrama, however, these extrinsic contrivances are allowable'; a significant reflection on the times.

Above is *The Old Chateau* at the Haymarket Theatre, 1854. This was a 'triangle' drama. Press comment was: 'It doubtless required great delicacy on the part of the dramatist to avoid inducing an unworthy sentiment... The accessories of the scene ... are in admirable keeping with the pathetic tragedy... Aided by such artistic effects, the curtain falls ... while the mind of the spectator is in a purely aesthetic state...' Again a comment on the times.

The Miller and His Men (above) is perhaps the great classic of all Victorian melodrama, and was certainly the dearly-beloved favourite of all possessers of toy theatres in the early days of the present century. It is here depicted as revived at the Haymarket in 1861, under Buckstone's management and with William Farren as Lothair. The explosion of the brigand's gunpowder store at the end is one of the great moments.

Below is a curious scene which appears (as indeed did other sensational sets) effective enough to have had plays written especially to exploit it. It is being used on this occasion for a Lyceum show under Madame Celeste entitled *The House on the Bridge of Notre Dame* in 1861. Its great feature was that it admitted a variety of actions simultaneously. But it had been used before for the melodrama of *Jonathan Bradford; or, The Murder at the Roadside Inn* at the Surrey Theatre in 1833.

A WILLIAMSON, DEL

An actor from France, Charles Albert Fechter, played Hamlet in 1861 at the Princess's Theatre and created an impression that was regarded as revolutionary in its time. 'English actors', claimed *The Illustrated London News*, 'aim but little at the strict impersonation of Shakespearean heroes. They, for the most part, take up with the conventional types... Mr. Fechter is content to depend on natural impulse.' This is something of a stricture upon Victorian actors in Britain; apparently a sense of freshness was sometimes missing. The critic goes on by saying of Fechter's performance: 'We can imagine an amateur of great talent or genius delivering himself to such a conception ... but scarcely a professional actor.' Perhaps this is one of the first indications of a realisation that the orthodox Victorian player might be grinding his work into a rut. The scenic effects of Fechter's productions were well

arranged in contemporary opinion, and the Victorian scene-painter was still unspoiled at the top of his skill. A drawing (above) by the distinguished scenic artist, William Telbin, shows something of the almost 'modern' conception in which Fechter staged his *Hamlet*.

Two years later, in a magazine edited by Charles Dickens called *All the Year Round*, an article appeared which attributed great things to Fechter; it said, 'Mr. Fechter has recently caused to be constructed in Great Britain, and out of materials supplied by the British timber-merchant, a stage upon a principle entirely different from any previously tried in this country.' He was said to have done away with the grooves and introduced the continental system of scene-changing, in which the wings and setpieces are carried on frames reaching down through slits in the stage-floor, and running on rails laid in the cellar below the stage. Not only the scenes on the stage itself were thus revised, but the hanging scenery above came in for a revolution. It will be possible to have, says the article, 'an interior shut in above with a ceiling . . .' and in these words the true box set is foretold. The greatest innovation, however, concerned the borders and backcloth : 'In open outdoor scenes' there was to be 'an unbroken canopy extending from a certain point behind the proscenium and high above it, over the stage, and away to where, at the extreme backward limit of the theatre, it mingles softly with the horizon. . .' It seems clear that here we have a reference to the technique of the 'cyclorama', that typical element of twentieth-century stage equipment. If this is so, then the drawing here reproduced showing Telbin's scene for Fechter as Hamlet meeting his father's ghost, is 'modern' indeed. It is almost certainly one of the earliest representations we have of a 'cyclorama set' on the English stage.

It is interesting, however, to find that the innovations did not apparently suit the Victorian public. By the time Irving took over the Lyceum in 1878, Fechter's new machinery had been done away with.

It is perhaps surprising that W. S. Gilbert's early work, before his epoch-making association with Arthur Sullivan in the Savoy operas, should have included typical examples of melodrama. Illustrated here is his *Dan'l Druce, Blacksmith*, produced at the Haymarket Theatre in 1876. The stirring line which the hero is delivering is 'Hands off! Touch not the Lord's gift,' from the end of Act I. The engraving, by the Dalziel Brothers, well records the robust style of acting.

This production (opposite above) of the old comedy, *Married for Money*, belongs to 1874, and it was then revived (as an afterpiece, that particular example of the almost profligate richness of the Victorian theatre programme) by the younger Charles Mathews at the Gaiety Theatre. A typical comment from *The Pictorial World* of the day runs: 'Altogether there is really an excellent entertainment at the cosy Gaiety now—three pieces every evening, and Mr. Mathews in two of them! What more can theatre-goers desire?'

If they could desire anything more, then that desire might be satisfied by the play below. This is a presentation, towards the end of the century, of a dramatisation of Mrs Henry Wood's novel *East*

Lynne, first published in 1861. It might claim to be called the most pathetic play of the era, and included the renowned lines from Madame Vine above her dying child (see *Dick's Standard Penny Plays*): 'Look at me, William. I am your mother! (*catches him in her arms. He says "Mother" faintly, and falls back dead in her arms*.)—he is dead! Oh, William! wake and call me mother once again! My child is dead!—my child is dead..!'

Victorian Scene-painting

Turning from scenic plays to the highly specialised task of producing the scenery, we pass into a strange mystery-world smelling strongly and characteristically of hot size. The major appliance in this world is the gigantic paint-frame, rising and falling through a slit in a specially-designed floor by means of a winch and counterweights, as shown on this page. Or alternatively, the frame might be fixed, and then the scenic artist was enabled to reach all parts of the great back-scenes by means of a rising and sinking bridge, or cradle, in front of the cloth, and in which he had to wind himself up and down, as at the Haymarket Theatre (opposite). Generally speaking, this vertical method of scene-painting was peculiar to the British scenic artist. On the continent the backcloths were spread flat on the floor of a vast studio, and the painter walked across them in slippers to paint the scene. The smaller British theatres could rarely spare sufficient space within their walls (nor money to rent space outside) for laying out cloths on the floor, and thus the vertical method became general. The amount of 'step back' available to the painter was sometimes very limited, and it was often extremely difficult to get an idea of the appearance of the whole effect until the cloth was rolled up, taken off the frame, carried to the stage, and hung in position. Then any but slight touching-up was impracticable. A scene-painter had, then, to have an exceptionally clear idea of what he was doing and what effect he wanted, and how to achieve that effect in a paint which changed tone considerably as it dried, and changed colour even more under the coloured lights of the stage.

Today there are few examples left of actual scenes by the Victorian scene-painters, but the Theatre Royal, Northampton, still proudly preserves (carefully rolled in linen) the act-drop which was painted for it by (so tradition goes) no less a person that the great Telbin himself. This photograph of the drop is reproduced on this page by the kind offices of the distinguished contemporary scene-designer of that theatre, Osborne Robinson. It is possibly worth remarking that all the folded drapery on this scene is painted on the flat canvas, and modelled by sheer skill.

On this page are two views of one and the same distemper sketch for a scene, by possibly the most brilliant of all late-Victorian scenic artists, Hawes Craven (whose full name was Henry Hawes Craven Green and who lived from 1837 to 1910). He was one of Irving's painters and also worked for Fechter at the Lyceum in 1863-4. The pictures illustrate what could be done with a 'transparency cloth'; above, it is lit from the front and presents a normal wood scene. When the front is dimmed and lights are brought up from behind (see below) the intriguing mystery of a sylvan evening appears—offering one of the distinct charms of Victorian 'stage illusion'.

The amateur theatre, too, had its scene-painters in the Victorian era. Some of them were highly ambitious, if not so accomplished. At Street School, in Somerset, there are still preserved a number of theatrical backcloths that were used by amateurs in late-Victorian times. Among them is a 'corridor cloth'—that indispensable stand-by scene for almost any play—which it is interesting to compare with the masterly drop on page 92; the drapery is in much the same conception. Framing the cloth are two pairs of plain, panelled wings which could serve equally as the walls of a palace-chamber set, and which have no relation decoratively to the backcloth whatever.

Opposite is a wood-and-lakeside scene from the same source, with the moon and the ripples in the water cut out and made transparencies for night effects. Below, is a group of fairly light-hearted comments from *Stage Whispers* on the scenic side of the contemporary theatre. No 1 gibes at the typical ship scene: 'A is a Sky Border. Splendid Atmospheric Effect. B and C are Wings, showing Gunwale and Sea-line of Horizon. They don't fit much, but no matter'. No 2 comments on the unsuitability of large palace-sets for small cottage-interiors. No 3 shows the wrong halves of two pairs of flats closed-in together. No 4 shows 'A Low Comedian, with no sense of perspective' having a 'lark with Distant Windmill'.

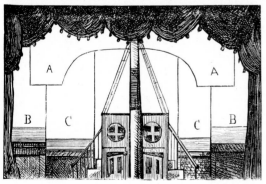

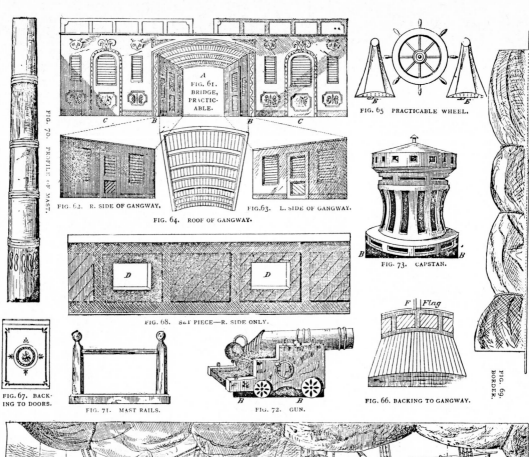

FIG. 70. PROFILE OF MAST.

FIG. 61. BRIDGE, PRACTICABLE.

FIG. 62. R. SIDE OF GANGWAY.

FIG. 64. ROOF OF GANGWAY.

FIG. 63. L. SIDE OF GANGWAY.

FIG. 65 PRACTICABLE WHEEL.

FIG. 73. CAPSTAN.

FIG. 68. SET PIECE—R. SIDE ONLY.

FIG. 67. BACKING TO DOORS.

FIG. 71. MAST RAILS.

FIG. 72. GUN.

FIG. 66. BACKING TO GANGWAY.

FIG. 69. BORDER.

Though the art of scene-painting was such a highly-developed speciality in the Victorian era, the lesser craft of making models of scenes was open to everyone, and was described in journals typical of the period, such as *Amateur Work*. On the opposite page are figures from a series of articles by Henry L. Benwell in 1884 on 'Practical Scene Painting for Amateurs', showing how the typical ship scene that we have noticed more than once was put together. The complication of details and set-pieces is considerable, and much care is given to perspective effect and to making suitable items 'practical', or capable of actually being used in the action. At the side of the upper diagram is shown a 'sail border' to frame-in the top of the scene. The lower picture gives a view of the finished set, with a notable example of 'horizon wings' (such as were gibed at on the previous page) framing the sides.

By the end of the century the 'pair of flats' was going out of favour and was being replaced by the backcloth hung from above. In practice this meant the end of scene-changing under the eyes of the audience; so it is that today we may have to wait some ten or fifteen minutes with the curtain down while the scene is changed behind. This falling curtain had its perils when much action took place on the old deep fore-stage, as is shown below in a joke from *Stage Whispers*. The prompter says to the actor, 'You're a-dying with your head outside the curtain. You'll have to die again higher up!' The details of scenery, side lights and curtain are clearly and accurately suggested.

G

Henry Irving and Others

The period draws to a close with a suitably pre-eminent Victorian, the first actor to bring the dignity of a knighthood to his profession for his work—Sir Henry Irving. He had many faces, if only one (very characteristic) body and voice; below is an old photograph showing him in *The Bells*; opposite above are two caricatures from *Stage Whispers*, one as 'The Dane' and the other as 'The Jew', and included in the accompanying note is the following: 'Had I not seen him . . . and only heard his demerits discussed by his detractors, I still think I should have been curious to see the man with the much-abused legs, who could not pronounce English properly, and from the door of whose theatre a crowd was turned away each night because there was not standing-room.' A great tribute.

Below is one of his most elaborately mounted productions, *Romeo and Juliet* at the Lyceum in 1882. Round the bier where Ellen Terry lies is a profusion of that detail that the Victorians had come to look for on the stage. Press comment included: '...one of the most admirable scenes...is the tomb'; and 'Admiration reaches a climax in the weird closing scene ...' This eerie vault was the design of William Telbin. The other designers of this outstanding show were Hawes Craven and William Cuthbert, with curtains painted by Walter Hann.

This scene of Queen Katherine's dream, from Irving's presentation of *Henry VIII* at the Lyceum in 1892, is particularly interesting to compare with the newspaper illustration of the same scene as it appeared some forty years earlier in Charles Kean's presentation (page 48). The use of a transparency in the backcloth, to show the angels descending, marks the persistence of tradition in such effects. Below is a spirited drawing by Hawes Craven of the castle interior for Irving's *Macbeth* at the Lyceum in 1888.

Irving's *King Lear* (Lyceum, 1892) was interesting in having the scene designs of the two regular scenic artists, Hawes Craven and Joseph Harker, first submitted for criticism to the aged and bed-ridden Ford Maddox Brown. He took exception to the primitive, Stonehenge-style of architecture they had adopted, and had it changed into the (surely less suitable?) 'classic' style that is shown in these two pictures. This was one of the very early examples of the design for a show coming from an outside artist, whose ideas the practical technicians of the theatre had to make into workable scenery. Today an artist who can both design and paint his scenery is relatively rare, and the scene-painter has had to become an executant contractor outside. Overleaf we glance at four notable contemporaries of Irving.

Edward William Godwin, father of Gordon Craig, was himself a scene designer of delicacy and originality. He was among those who began to move away from the over-profuseness of Victorian scenery. In 1886 he designed a setting for Todhunter's *Helena in Troas* at the theatre known as Hengler's Circus (where the Palladium now stands), which was a surprisingly forward-looking example of open staging (above).

Joseph Harker, another of the major, versatile scenic artists, not only worked for Irving but produced a fresh-style setting of a houseboat on the Thames for the first play of a new playwright, James Barrie, entitled *Walker, London*, presented at Toole's Theatre, Charing Cross, in 1892 (below).

Among the more significant of the Victorian innovators was the producer, William Poel, who restored Shakespeare's scripts to their full form and attempted to present his plays, not in cut versions with elaborate scenery, but entire and on the style of stage for which they were written. Above is his presentation of *Measure for Measure* at the Royalty Theatre in 1893.

Below is reproduced an old photograph of the setting made by William Telbin for Sir George Alexander's production of *Much Ado about Nothing* at the St James's Theatre in 1898; by contrast, one of the most elaborately built sets ever used to stage a Shakespeare scene.

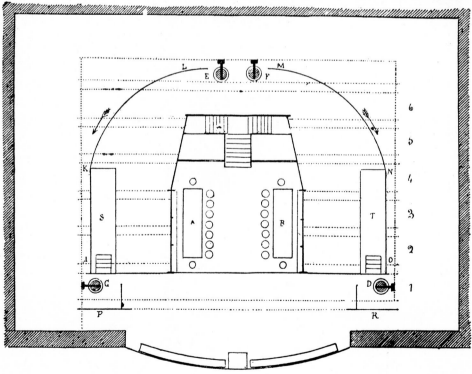

The 'Entortilationists'

We conclude this very brief survey with a curiosity. The English player was renowned through Europe at this time for one particular style of entertainment in which he was said to surpass the world —the specialist and exceedingly exacting technique of acrobatic trick-work. The early players of the century had produced some fine families of trap-workers, but by the eighties a troupe had arisen, calling itself the Hanlon-Lees, whose skill and daring and, over and above, whose startling ability to agonise yet entrance an audience, made the *Times* critic in 1880 willing to speak of their shows and of 'some burst of passion at the Lyceum' (where Irving was playing) in the same breath. They had taken for themselves the marvellous name of 'Entortilationists'. In one of their confections, called *The Journey to Switzerland* (*Le Voyage en Suisse*), they set out by showing the departure of their ship from the quay. The scene is preserved for us here in the lithograph opposite. And fortunately there is also preserved a plan of how this scene was made up (opposite below). It shows that the quayside houses were on two curved panorama cloths which rolled away to the front as the ship sailed out into the open water. Once clear of land, the ship ran into that delight of Victorian audiences—a storm at sea (above). But not only did the ship toss on the waves; part of its stern slid away to show the interior and there, in ideal conditions for agility, the Hanlon-Lees flung a banquet and held a concert with every opportunity for sensation—one of them even taking a header through the specially constructed piano.

A later scene was even more fantastic and hair-raising. It began quietly enough with a guest being shown into a Parisian hotel bedroom by candlelight (see above). But the scenery for the room was specially prepared in a remarkable number of details. In a French study of trick scenery by Georges Moynet called *Trucs et Décors*, a diagram is given of the construction of this scene viewed from the back (below). There are twelve different kinds of trap in the walls. For a beginning, the traveller's boots, when he took them off to retire, walked away across the room and up the wall and vanished into the ceiling (opposite above). The rest of the scene was a nightmare of scampering demons whom

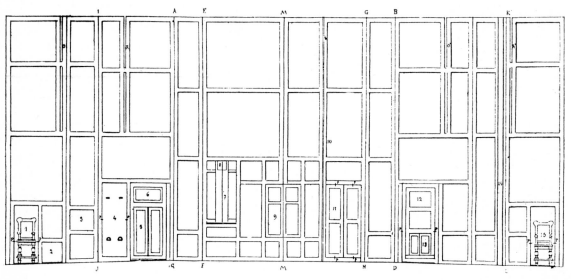

he could never catch; and every device of the Victorian theatre was worked into this one show in such a way that, when they played in Paris, Emile Zola said of the Hanlon-Lees that they 'laid bare, with a wink, a gesture, the entire human breast'. Such an act is clearly impossible to describe, but some further details can be found in *Life and Letters Today*, in the articles 'Entortilationists' by Thomas Walton, April, 1941, and 'Vision of Leaps' by the present writer, September, 1941.

Finale

Bibliography

The present book has not dealt in any detail with the stage personalities of the Victorian period nor with what are known as 'the minor theatres'; Mr George Nash of the Theatre Collection, the Victoria and Albert Museum, is at present working on a manuscript to cover these subjects, and his bibliography will form a useful supplement to the following as far as they are concerned.

As regards aspects of the Victorian theatre treated in this book, the architecture may be studied in:
Buckle, J. G. *Theatre Construction and Maintenance* (1888)
Mander, Raymond and Mitchenson, Joe. *The Theatres of London* (1963) and *London's Lost Theatres* (1968)
Sachs, Edwin O. *Modern Opera Houses and Theatres*, 3 vols (1896-9)
Sherson, Errol. *London's Lost Theatres of the XIXth Century* (1925)

Stage machinery is dealt with in:
Contant, Clément. *Parallèle des principaux théâtres modernes de l'Europe*, 2 vols (Paris 1859) (this, though a French work, has a valuable section on 'The English System')
Moynet, Georges. *Trucs et Décors* (Paris 1893) (again a French book but with special reference to English procedure)
Southern, Richard. *Changeable Scenery, its Origin and Development in the British Theatre* (1952)

Scenery and scene-painting are discussed in:
Harker, Joseph. *Studio and Stage* (1924)
Lloyds, Frederick. *Practical Guide to Scene Painting and Painting in Distemper* (nd, ? 1875)
Benwell, Henry L. 'Practical Scene-painting for Amateurs', 31 articles appearing serially in *Amateur Work* from December 1884

General works on other relevant aspects are:
Disher, M. Wilson. *Blood and Thunder* (1949)
Fitzgerald, Percy. *The World behind the Scenes* (1881)
Rowell, George. *The Victorian Theatre* (1956)
Speaight, George. *The History of the English Toy Theatre* (1969)
Vardac, A. N. *Stage to Screen* (Cambridge 1949) (a useful study of the technical theatre of the period, particularly stressing American sources)

A detailed survey of the drama of the period is in the relevant volumes of:
Nicoll, Allardyce. *Nineteenth Century Drama*

In addition to the above books, certain illuminating contemporary comments may be found in magazine articles etc, especially in:
Knight's *The Penny Cyclopaedia . . . of Useful Knowledge* (1842) under 'Scenepainting'
All the Year Round, 31 October 1863 ('A New Stage Stride')
The Architectural Review, August 1946 ('Interesting Matter relating to the scenery, decorations etc. of the Theatre Royal, Tackett Street, Ipswich'; article by Richard Southern describing an important manuscript scrapbook in the Ipswich Public Library)
The Art Journal, vol for 1853, p 228, and vol for 1873, p 27
Life and Letters Today, April 1941 ('Entortilationists' by Thomas Walton) and September 1941 ('Vision of Leaps' by Richard Southern)
The Magazine of Art, vol for 1889, pp 94 and 199 (articles by W. Telbin junior on scenery)
The Theatre, March 1884 ('Scenery, Dresses and Decoration' by Godfrey Turner)

Acknowledgements

The illustrations for this book have been selected from prints and photographs in the combined Richard Southern Collection and Drama Department Collection in the University of Bristol, with the exception of the frontispiece and those on pages 98 and 102 (top) for which see below.

The originals forming the subjects of the illustrations on pages 18, 24, 40, 41, 42, 43, 44, 45, 46, 49, 66, 87, 93, 98, 100 (bottom), 102, 103 (top) are in the Theatre Collection of the Victoria and Albert Museum, London; that on page 51 in the Guy Little Collection, Victoria and Albert Museum; that on page 92 belongs to the Northampton Repertory Players Ltd; and those on pages 94, 95 (top) to Street School, Somerset. The illustrations on pages 12, 13, 14, 15, 30 (bottom), 44, 45, 49, 72-3, 75, 93, 104, 105, 106, 107, 108 are from a series of film-strips by the present author, on *The History of the English Theatre*, published by Common Ground (1951) Ltd.

The frontispiece is from a model in the Guildford Museum, reproduced from a colour transparency in the Victoria and Albert Museum reproduction department.

Index